The White Cockade

Catholic Poetry and Verse

By

Charles A. Coulombe

"So up with shout and out with blade,
We'll stand or fall with the White Cockade!"
 - Irish Ballad

Arcadia
MMIX

Library of Congress Catalog Card Number 90-82476

ISBN 0-9842365-0-3

All Rights Reserved

Future rights to the eight pen-and-ink illustrations are
retained by the artist, Ryan Brookhart

© Text and poems copyright 2009 by Charles Coulombe

Manufactured in the United States

PREFACE:

TWENTY YEARS AFTER

Poetry is a young man's game. That is not to say that older people (and women) can't write fine poetry. They can and do. But there is something about a man's youth --- his late teens and early twenties that lends itself to poetry. As my friend Richard Cowden-Guido puts it, "It is easy to be interesting when you are young; you'll spend the rest of your life struggling against being a bore!" It is obvious that most of us are not equal to the struggle. Dr. Johnson preferred the sins of youth to those of age, because they are not coupled with sanctimony.

It is not merely that one is physically stronger or more attractive in one's youth than he will likely become; it is that everything is new --- romance, politics, even war. The blush is not yet off the apple. Ideas are important, as are art, conversation, wine and moonlight. Who has not had an all-night bull session in college, at the end of which the world's problems are solved? When you are young you believe that, given the right chance, you can conquer the world!

And what a world it is --- filled with joy and horror, with wrongs to be righted and avenged, with glorious causes to be fought for! "To be young was very Heaven!" Shelley said of the age of Revolution in the 18th century, and so, in some aspects, it always is for the young. Their ardor and passion can lead them on the High Crusade --- or into the Red Guards.

But the flip side is one of fear and doubt. What is my place in the world? Will I ever find it? Will I grow old without success? Will my life be a waste? Does she really love me? Is she the one? Will I ever find love? --- and on and on. Middle Age may be duller and less fiery, but generally, for good or ill, those questions have been answered.

So it is that the poems in *The White Cockade* were all written in my youth; some when I was a cadet at New Mexico Military Institute, others when I was struggling as a comic in Hollywood, still others when I was a novice writer looking for my voice. In earlier days, the great shadow was the Mordor-like Soviet Union; in the later poems, the joy and anticipation launched by the fall of that "Evil Empire" was uppermost, and for very different reasons I felt like Shelley.

All of that has changed, since, and both of the political sources of fear and elation have passed away, taking my youth with them. This writer has generated oceans of print since he penned the lines you are about to read, and his contents and discontents are those of Middle Age. Yet, when reading the afterword, he finds his views in art, religion, and politics have not changed. As the Russian song says, "oh my friend, we're older, but no wiser, for in our hearts our dreams are still the same."

Indeed they are. I've not written poetry in two decades, but the impulses that inspired these remain, and I still enjoy reading these. More importantly, many of those who were infants when these words written are young men now, and quite a few profess to have been inspired by them. A higher compliment cannot be paid to a poet.

The White Cockade

Every book of poetry is an adventure shared by the reader and the writer; and so we begin. But I will send you off a bit from one of my favorite anonymous ballads "Tom O' Bedlam's Song," that epitomizes to me the quest that all of us who live must undertake:

> With a host of furious fancies
> Whereof I am commander,
> With a burning spear and a horse of air,
> To the wilderness I wander.
> By a knight of ghostes and shadowes
> I summon'd am to tourney
> Ten leagues beyond the wild world's end.
> Methinks it is no journey.

Charles A. Coulombe
Arcadia, California
24 September 2009
Our Lady of Ransom

Aspirations

The March-Warden's Song

I ride the King's highway, wherever I go,
   Relentless, regardless of friend or of foe.
Ye ghoulish horrors that prowl by night,
   Beware or be tasted by sword-blade so bright

Though wild, deserted, this province I sing,
   Belongs yet by right to my master the King.
Further yet from His Majesty's siege
   Is granted in fief by Imperial Liege.

The whole thing witnessed with ineffable hope
   By their master and mine, our sovereign Lord Pope.
But far are those who hold it in fee,
   This forested border is watched over by me.

The wild wood-woses who dwell in the land
   Though looking like men, cannot understand.
Living like cattle born without souls
   Drag out their existence like tormented trolls.

Once all this province was lovely and fair,
   Its people contented, its knights without care.
Neglect and treachery smothered its good,
   Over green farmland grew up this wood.

Over the border the evil things came,
   Ogres, bogles, things without name.
The stones of roads the King had laid
   Grew over with bushes, became unmade.

The White Cockade

Taliessin and Dante found their way out,
   Most though were caught, lacking a scout.
Their witless descendants, the woses are here,
   Too witless and feckless to even know fear

Of the demon creatures that restlessly prowl
   When all are asleep, save the night owl.
My father's house was filled with song,
   There fires were bright and joy was long.

But summons came from His Majesty's Court
   Asking for aid where his long arm was short.
He sent me here to maintain good order,
   Alone without aid to warden the border.

Now, when a wose learns how to think
   Or a traveler lost in a bog starts to sink,
I help them out of this terrible waste
   Back to the road to leave in great haste.

This forest is deep, its boundaries are wide.
   Undaunted, alone I gradually ride.
But no matter how gaily I warble and sing,
   No messenger comes from the court of the King.

Nearby is a bishop who lives in a tower.
   We chat now and then for a day or an hour.
Other knights too sometimes ride this way,
   But of news from the Court can none of them say.

Yet I still believe in the King and his might,
   One day he shall come to save us from night.
This land yet is his till he comes back again,
   For him will I hold it, and battle his bane.

Aspirations

Ye ghoulish horrors that prowl by night,
   Beware! Or be tasted by sword-blade so bright.
Relentless, regardless of friend or of foe,
   I ride the King's Highway, wherever I go!

The White Cockade

For the White Rose

All Kings and all pretenders,
wherever you may be,
the land itself remembers
though we are far from thee.

You Counts and Knights and Barons
who served your God and King,
fear not the modern charons
who scorn their honor, sing

Of modern age's wonders
joys our science brought,
care not for bloody blunders
and evil that they wrought

All through the world's vast waters
the Monarchs sent their men
who ended Heathen slaughters
made salvation within ken

Of savage tribes and races.
To our South-west the King of Spain
sent Friars from their places
who worked and died in pain.

His Majesty of France indeed
the rivers took in fief,
Blackrobe, trapper, with great speed
converted brave and Chief.

The White Cockade

Even Britain's Sovereign cold
displayed his Royal worth,
dispatched minions sure and bold
to found our land of birth.

He who reigned in Sweden's north
sent all that he could spare,
brave Swedes for him sallied forth
and settled Delaware.

But facing revolution's frown,
the Monarch's call so loud,
for brave swords to help the crown
against the maddening crowd.

The Jacobites for Royal James
and Bonnie Charles as well,
the Carlists fought with Spanish names
while Chouans tasted Hell.

The brave emerged from old Vendee
and died at Quiberon
or fought with great old Duc Condé
or fell at bold Toulon.

And Hofer up in High Tyrol
fought his Emperor's foe
feared not to pay the awful toll
before they laid him low.

In Russia's far off blinding snows
the Whites fought for their Tsar,
and though the Country's lost in woe,
their glory none can mar.

Ethiopia, Laos, Iran
all had their Paladins
Vietnam, Afghanistan,
remind us of our sins.

I beg the King who reigns above
that to me may be shown
how to fight with savage love
for altar, and for throne.

After the '45

The News came in from Glenfinnan Crag
   That Bonnie Prince Charlie had raised up his flag.
Son Jamie came in with temper red-hot
   And fed me my dinner from the old iron pot.

"So, da," he said, "it's started again,
   Young Charlie Stuart will bring us more pain.
We will march, we will lose, he'll leave us between
   Like his father left you there, back in 'Fifteen."

For my darling Jamie to speak like a Whig,
   So brave and so braw, to act like a pig
It cut me to hear, to have such a one
   Speak with my faint heart, him my own son

"Your Grandsire marched with Bonnie Dundee,
   His sire with Montrose, to die by the sea.
I was at Sherrifmuir, back in Fifteen,
   All the drawn claymore's silvery sheen.
Had I not been your namesake's great pride
   Your ma would never have sat by my side."

"Oh, da," he said, with a trembling voice,
   "Why must I make this terrible choice
To leave yourself and the maiden I love,
   Go fight for James Edward's right to his glove?"

"Those that God loves to keep in His sight
Are men who will dare to struggle for right."
Jamie agreed, said he would go,
Was off to the army with morning's first glow.

Jamie alone was brought back again,
    To rest in the yard with our holy slain.
Our hope once bloomed, now it has fled.
    At Culloden it lies with bones of the dead.
Dora will not have him to keep as her lord,
    Never his bairns will play by my board.
Withered alike are love and good deeds
    While I lie here telling my beads.

The Pope heads the Church, James Edward is King!
    May all the cursed Whigs from the gallows soon swing!
If I pass Brig O' Doom, Purgatory Fire,
    Arrive at the place where saints play the lyre,
Gladly will I bow to James, seventh King
    Unto great God Hosannas will sing.
Catch Jamie's blue eye with my sad one of red,
    Kiss the fair hair on Jamie's young head.

The White Cockade

Stabat Mater Dolorosa

Weeping there, the Mother stands above
    The altar at Soledad,
Ebon-draped, inside that valley where
    The very wind is sad.
And its blowing through the mountains
    Like the cries of souls long crushed,
Tells the tale of dreams of Empire turned
    By treason into dust.

Truth and glory from Iberia
    Came into the valley dim,
Brought the light of love to Christendom's
    Northern rim.
In the way that up the rivers, through
    The valleys with great pain,
Was brought the splendor that was France,
    And glory that was Spain.
Loyal saints and martyrs served their Kings
    And served their God.
Their souls indeed found Heaven while
    Their bodies fed the sod!
Though the French have gone from Vincennes,
    The Spanish left Tubac,
Their spirit lives in San Antone
    And the Fortress of Quebec.
The Churches of New Orleans
    And the Churches of Carmel
Still show the old defiance of the
    English and of Hell.
Though the Godless Yankee moneyman
    In the end have won the day,
From across the sea came immigrants

The White Cockade

   Who believed the ancient way.
But the sons of Poland, and the Swiss,
   The men of Italy,
Could not resist the horrid blight
   Which claimed to set me free.
The Mass is stripped of all
   That splendor, truly due a King
Collared fools have muddied
   The Sacramental spring.
Clerical opportunists prate of love,
   Communal joy,
But they know them as mere slogans,
   A rather useful ploy.

To think of Father Serra and the
   Pioneers of Faith,
Will bring to mind our clergy's
   Losing of God's Grace.
Though Our Lady cries in Soledad,
   Where the winds do moan,
On my honor, Lady Mary,
   You do not weep alone.

Death in Paris

I have lived three years
    On the rue de Cabanis
And find myself dry.

Walking down cobbled streets,
    Blue-and-White signs that
Tell me where I am,
    But not where I am.

The people, yes the people,
    Kindly old ones, lively young,
I laugh with them, but not
    With them.

Why? I have love and what I want.
    A ride on the metro
Will take me to the Louvre,
    Or the Guard at Elysee.

I left my native land to find – what?
    It was not there,
Nor in Paris, City of light.
    But then –

Watching the Cadre Noir at paces
    In Saumur.
Hearing the carrillon of Notre Dame.
    What hope?

The White Cockade

I kneel here at the altar
   Of St. Nicolas-du-Chardonnet.
I smell incense – *miserere mei*,
   Great God, give a sign!

Absalom

The fire on his brow of dedication
Fanned the flames of my own vocation.

When he would elevate the Host
He seemed indeed to have most

Of Grace that Heaven gives a Priest
In this age when Faith is quite least

And passion too of modern wisdom
But Priests forget the Kingdom.

Though many sins one can hide,
The one to slay a Priest is evil pride.

All others follow in its wake,
Lead the Priest to burning lake.

I cry to Heaven,
               And I curse
                            to
                                 Hell,

The glory has gone out of Israel.

A Note of Dissent

I must admit that I often dream
   Of the glimmering light of the Old Regime.
In my secret garden grows
   The Lily and the fair White Rose.
Over all, the mournful cry
   Of the Double-Eagle fills the sky.
In this day of grenade and tank,
   When real power lies in the Bank,
Such hoping for a muse of fire
   Runs counter to approved desire.
But still I hope a time will come,
   Before my tale of years is done,
When exiled to the realm of dream
   Is the souless face of the New Regime.

Observations

In Memoriam Vini Antiqui
To New Mexico Military Institute

The lads with whom I drank my wine,
when all the world seemed grand and fine,
In the days when we were young
before our youth on life was hung
Have scattered now throughout the world,
their manhood's standards with joy unfurled.
Some have followed Venus, some love Mars,
some for business, and its paper wars.
But once commerce and affairs of state
could not with drinking songs quite rate.
We told our secrets of love and horror
and ran the case with collegiate ardor.
Drinking and eating o'er a filled-up table,
the greatest was he with the finest fable.
Although we none of us yet are old,
we can feel age's cold.
And nothing seems as it did appear,
before the rush to build career.
When all the world seems strange and odd,
for that time, I thank my God,
when the world seemed grand and fine,
to the lads and me as we drank our wine.

To Baron Corvo

Corvo, I wish greatly I had lived
to know you. It seems though,
had I done so, I would wish
'twere as it is right now!

On the Plebiscite in Quebec

Arise! Land of my Fathers!
   Zion in the New World! Let
      not the chains of conquest
         bind you! Poor, primitive, better
            far, than follow Brittania's sons
down the road to death. Let
   the day come when you may
      cast off foreign ways, and
         gladly chant, "Ourselves alone!"

Birth of a Nation

Oh, see, Uranus rise in the sky,
there is a monster born,
Zimbabwe, the name is a lie,
Succubus-born of the carcass of Rhodesia.

Obituary: Private Terence O'Neill

O'Neill was his Gaelic name,
Scion of proud chiefs of Ulster;
The land his grandfather left.
   When he was drunk his mates
Carried him, and said, "Ah well,
      He's Irish."
But never had he seen the land of
    His father's calling home.

Land of the valiant Red-Branch Knights,
    Land of the Roisin Dubhe.
  When he said "Erin Go Bragh!" he
    meant a mystic fairy land,
     East of the Sun,
     West of the Moon.
His speech was more of Bow than Derry,
    Cockney than proud Antrim.

  For lack of money, he joined
    the army of
      the queen

Off to Crossmaglen, Britain's Vietnam.
He found his heritage at the end of a
    bullet from the bold
        IRA

His mother said her Rosary, wept freely
    at the news.
"Private Terence O'Neill, killed in action,
In the service of Her Majesty the Queen."

London in 1895

The Knights still ride against the foe,
   German flappers do the Charleston yet,
      Sherlock Holmes sees the game's afoot,
         And its always London in 1895.

We are all riding on the Orient Express,
   Down to New Orleans, for Ivanhoe is waiting.
      Beatrice beckons, with Terry and his pirates.
         And it's always London, in 1895.

The summers that have never been,
   Outside the King's house in Cair Paravel,
      Riding with Arthur, Galahad, Lancelot
         And it's always London, in 1895.

When the eye, the mind, are black and blind,
   The heart and soul see through,
      They pierce reality's hermetic wrap
         To where it's always London, in 1895.

A Tourist in Port Malheur

Jolly faces, filled with hate,
Black and Brown fill the square.
Tourists laugh and drink 'till late,
enjoy the island without care.

Breezes cool, from off the sea
blow past Kings House without cease
by staid Christ Church and Ste. Marie
to my table where I sit at peace.

Immune from poverty, horror's yoke,
like bird snatching rodent from a palm,
I drink my rum-and-coke.
Despite the dangers I am calm.

Though here the Zombie walks at night
the loup-garou may stalk his prey
Obi cults who shun the light
push red rebellion into day.

But while this Island teems with pain,
terror that makes brave men shrink,
my hotel door still has a chain,
and I still have a drink.

Lament of Mr. Sangreuse

Do branches crack in Yvelines?
To there I dare not wander.
   Elves that dance in Broceliande
   Shall see me there no longer.

Beneath the Dryad's calling trees
No more shall I go riding.
   Desolate the Demoiselle d'Ys
   For lack of my confiding.

I will not hunt with Duke Robert
For stags, wolves or moors.
   For he is dead, and young Gilbert
   Cannot track the spoors.

Now I wear a business suit
And step the modern dance,
   Yet I recall the harp and flute,
   The glory that was France.

All must age – yet I do not.
It is not of my doing
   All my friends of old must rot
   Whilst I my curse am ruing.

Duke Robert's love was sweet indeed.
Alas, his blood was sweeter.
   In my thirsting sanguine need,
   I slew Gilbert and Peter.

The White Cockade

Adieu to you, fair land of France
Time crashes on unbroken.
   Immune am I to fair romance,
   My secret stays unspoken.

Centuries wearier than the last
Have not stopped me from seeking,
   An answer to my gory past,
   An end to evil wreaking.

But Elves that dance in Broceliande
Shall see me there no longer.
   Though branches crack in Yvelines
   To there I dare not wander.

The Phantom Wood

The woods are deep, and still resound
 With trumpet blasts and calls of hound.
The huntsman's quarry, stag and fox,
 Elude his chase through rills and rocks.

There! A wolf crawls from his lair,
 Out for the deer, he stalks a pair.
Osprey dives for his little prey –
 Sad field mouse, with fur of grey.

Duke Robert is hunting with hound and horse,
 His fire-eyed stallion streaks over gorse.
He is the King's guest, at Louvre takes ease
 Whilst courting the fair Demoiselle d'Ys

But Duke Robert is dead these five hundred years.
 Ma Demoiselle d'Ys is dust with her tears.
Gone are the wolf and the boar and the deer,
 Gone are serf and valiant peer.

I must be dreaming in this little park,
 My head is affected by oak, ash, and bark.
But where is my suit of imitation suede?
 Why am I dressed in old brocade?

Dark Waters

"We must pass through dark waters
  Before we reach the sweet."
Said Van Helsing as with heavy heart
  And aching feet,
He stalked through city, moor, crypt,
  And fen,
To catch Bloodsucker in his
  Dreary den.

In sad noblesse did Royal Flavia
  With tears recall
At storied Strelsau, "Ah dear, if
  Love were all,"
Then bowing to the regal duties thrust
  By fate,
Forsook her love for reasons of the
  Crowns's estate.

Most loyal Beren who took Tinuviel for
  Good or ill,
With her aid braving death to wrest,
  A silmaril,
Was by strength of Romance
  And love's might
Allowed to conquer by fierce combat
  Cruel night.

All indeed well learned the lesson
   Of love's law,
That those who love must struggle with
   The flaw
Which from the time of Adam's
   Sinful mirth
Has clouded those who breathe upon
   The Earth.

So we who separated are for now by
   Mournful fate,
Yet are not burdened by duty or
   High estate,
May through love snatch victory
   From defeat,
And pass through these dark waters
   To the sweet.

The White Cockade

In the New Alexandria

She called me from the world's last night
    On the phone her voice thrilled with fright,
Shattering my happy, quiet reverie
    Stirring up my harshly battered memory.
To me in rending tones she pled
    That those round her were drugged undead.
Trapped she was in night-club plight,
    Would I please lead her toward the light?
In drinks and darkness did she grope –
    My voice, though, gave a ray of hope.
Reminded her of brighter days,
    Made her think of purer ways.

My soul was sent by her sad voice
    Back to the time before my choice
Ended my nights on L.A.s streets,
    Glad refuge sought beneath the sheets
From folk whose layer of moral dirt
    Served them to hide the mortal hurt
Of Godless days and empty nights
    Among the City's famous sights.
Out of Time, and out of Space,
    My hapless friends ran their race.

In those days I lived on dreams,
    Grateful for the grace that streams
From scarlet altar vigil light,
    Reflected from the monstrance bright.

The White Cockade

At last I took my sword of fire,
    On Grail-Quest I left the mire
Which yet holds many whom I love;
    Upon whom rests no healing dove.
For them the struggle must be fought
    Against the Lord of darkest Naught.

"My dear," I said in tone reserved,
    "You have not had what you deserved.
Let us dine upon another day,
    To speak of molding finer clay."
She agreed, rang off the phone,
    So, we parted quite alone.

From a Cynic Neighbor

Oh, I sit quite tranquil,
        And sip my tea,
One of few things you people
        Brought to repay the rape
Of Mars.

Yes, I suppose you could
      Not be restrained.
Your Godless new world's might
      Could not have less.

Godless, yes. Yet you called
        Us idolators!
        Never mind.
Our people began to die before
        Yours were
        Born.

The measured tone of our decay
      Gave quiet to our lives
And grandeur to our fall.

So, you brought the careful benefits:
        Boot, baton, and whip!
This to give us meaning, purpose.
        Not least, incentive!
            How considerate!

The White Cockade

This Tyria of ours, Mars you name her, rust-red for a
      Million years –
     Blood-red in
       twenty.
   Tombs of our kings – sideshows.
   Temples of our God – circuses.
     But Elysium's pyramids defy their
billboards.

God has quarantined. No other worlds can you reach
across the sea of stars.
You are marooned upon your silent planet,
Only ourselves within reach to torment.
God will not permit it forever. No, no, and again, no.

   I have heard a mad poet,
In Farad, which guards the road
   To Illinois, gateway of the gods.
He played triumphantly, sang a song
    Of War.

       "Strangers will be slaughtered,
       Our hosts will be caught stars."

Ah well, I sit quite tranquil, and sip my tea.

The Prayer of the Publican

Oh Father, thanks for making me
    Not as that two-faced Pharisee!
He gives alms and rings a bell
    I give none, but wish folk well.

He fasts for holiness in men's eyes,
    I feast on all that money buys.
He keeps the law that Moses brought
    I hold that foolishness for naught.

In short, he's a foul hypocrite,
    And I a holy reprobate.
He practices good by Temple Wall;
    I don't practice good at all.
Thank you, I am no Pharisee,
    When all is said, I worship me.

Self-Epitaph

I was not over generous – true,
my charity perhaps not over-well.
Who but me should I love, who?
I think it unfair to be in Hell.

Conclusions

Conclusions

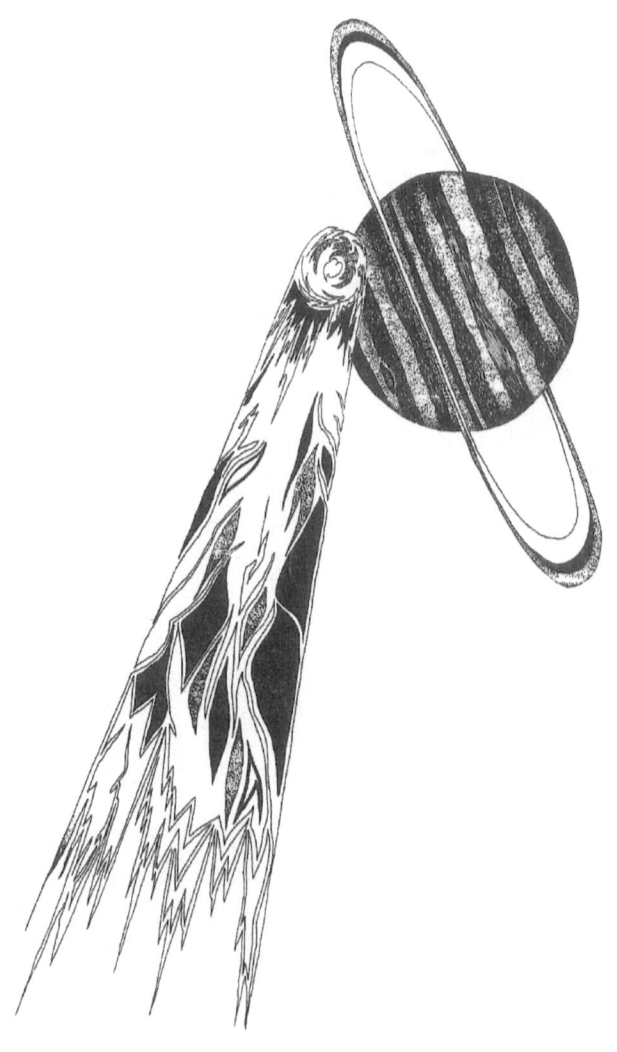

In the Year of the Comet

The old man's eyes of flashing blue
   twinkled as he stirred our stew.
"Never have you seen such as then,
   when the comet came in Nineteen-ten.

"The tail lit up the sky at night,
   it was hard to believe it could be so bright.
We spoke of it often in the years before
   the end of our world in the first great war.

"Oh, such marvelous times we had,
   such wondrous things to make us glad.
A waltz, white tied after dark,
   once I saw the Emperor in the park.

"All things progress, was our dream
   which ended rudely in 'fourteen'.
For years I worked in the same department
   and as reward I've this apartment.

This time the comet won't be so bright,
   it cannot pierce our modern night."

On a Darkling Plain

I say the world is dreadful and dark,
    Which cause some, perhaps, to remark,
That I must be a horrid Manichee,
    All caught up in duality.
But not all is bad that walks in flesh
    Nor is all good that has none to thresh.
This we may see from that Demon brood
    Enslaved by Suleiman-ben-Daoud,
Or from some fresh-faced country lad.
    Whose lass's smile makes so glad.
With her does a joyous advance
    At harvest home's rustic dance.
There is no nectar quite like wine.
    Drunk with friends from a better time.
But horrid things of bestial state
    Wait outside the mystic gate.
Should they hear a human's call
    Those hounds of night charge and maul
The barrier our kindly God has put
    To keep us safe from slime and soot
That Night's Black Agents put
    Wherever they set their odious claws.
They feel unbound by all the laws
    That humans in their folly break.
It is not for Our Lady's sake
    That Bishops will their churches bared
Or that like bloody wolves well laired
    Governments assist to murder young.
It's not for love of Him who once was hung
    Upon the Cross, that men crucify the Host,
Profaning Him with unclean touch and boast.
    But over this dark plain of Death's avarice

The White Cockade

This world of sacerdotal cowardice,
   Through fog and darkness of the mind
I see the stars that spite of evil shine.
   From ruined altars grows effulgent light
Enough in time to drown the darkest night,
   Now you who bear the Catholic name,
And follow Him who cured the lame.
   Remember Chivalry, try the same,
Perhaps you'll gain an equal fame.

Night in New Bedford

'Tis twilight in New Bedford-town,
and all is still and deep,
the day from that old Yankee town
has left and gone to sleep.
all is quiet on the wharf,
gone are sounds of day,
gone the whalers from the wharf,
the ships from Buzzards Bay.
A new decade has arrived,
(peradventure) it may stir
New Bedford from its sleep,
with a sounding crashing whir.

The Wild Hunt

All heads turn when the hunt goes by
  As baying hounds with flashing eye
    Precede the hunters all on horse,
      Men and Women in hysteric course.
        Chief Huntsman loudly blows the horn,
          The hunters by blood's passions torn
            In woods along in life's midway
              Pursue the unseen unknown prey
            Some by burning lust are led,
          They seek the quarry in barren bed.
        Others strive to kill their fear
      With poisoned arrow of career.
    All along the darkened path,
  They chase the game with mounting wrath,
Through drugs or drinks to quiet soul
  They stalk or speed to hidden goal
    Many are guided by Heaven's stars,
      High Magic's might, or Art of Mars.
        Those who themselves above the race
          Oft hurry fastest in savage pace
            With reddened, face, puffing breath
              They seek to cheat the ranger death
            No son of Adam is at all immune,
          All chase the quarry beneath the moon.
        Perhaps the answer might be known
      By Him Who holds the Altar-throne.
    But He's unpleasant, much too blunt,
  Unlike the Master of the Hunt.
So with the grinning Huntsman Scratch
  Through forest dark and briar-patch
    The Wild Hunt goes on and on.
      None know the quarry agreed upon,

But all insist it must be done.
For All will profit when 'tis won.
And so it goes from year to year,
With laughter, sorrow, strength and fear.
Father to son, daughter to girl,
Always replaced, the hunters whirl.
We may think ourselves too good,
Yet gladly join them in the Wood.
You say on death you cast cold eye?
All heads turn when the Hunt goes by.

50   *Conclusions*

Shadowland

I have spent the years of my existence
   With a blood-induced persistence
   In a strange New England of the soul -
Poe or Lovecraft cast the role.
With the old familial band
   I have lived in Shadowland.
In a set with Gothic towers
   Eidolons and Eldritch powers
   Wise old ones who surely know,
   Unearthly things that walk the snow.
The wild calling of the loon
   In ancient woodlands beneath the moon.
Though all I own is in a crate
   I carry close beside my fate.
A light has pierced my gloomy dark,
   On my soul has burned a mark -
But the carrier soon must go
   I must follow, or else know
That for all my talk so grand
   I bind myself in Shadowland.

Credo

Robber Barons and border Lords
Giant's Rings in Elven hoards
Venison sweet with blood-red win
Mystic wizards of ancient line
Wise old monks in woolen hoods
Fairy Kings in deep green woods
A golden cup to heal all ills
Loathsome things among the hills.

Arthur faces Mordred le mal,
Roland Stands at Roncesvalles.
You say the modern day's unfurled?
I'll take my stand in the older world.

The Ghost Book

In midst of all, have I learned at last,
Present is embedded in the past.
Sages say that the tree is bent
As the seedling is by nature sent.

Hunting, riding, friends I have had
Race cross my memory with visage glad.
The evil I have had to do,
What was good with what was true

Conspire to arrange my life
In pattern of symbolic strife;
Against its parts to fight, to strain
Between my spirit and my brain.

My dead relations rise to warn
Of betrayal; the coming storm
They rise within my fevered head,
So perhaps I'll thank the dead

Or curse them for the living fire
Which charts both duty and desire
But does not let man live as men
The wanderings in swamp and glen,

Verbal lashings of dear friends
Who food good, yes, honest ends
Try to share my private Hell;
Private Paradise as well.

Who try to soothe my riotous heart,
In internal battles take my part.
But these fierce skirmishes inside
Emerge from an unknown high tide

That crashes hard against the rocks
My father built to bind the shocks
That buffet one who crawls on Earth,
Armed but with anger, and with mirth.

If to my friends I am sometimes cruel,
Their love for me is still the jewel
I treasure. But the echoing past
Must hold me as my life is cast.

Of Ancient blood was I once born,
My greatest fear, ancestral scorn.
Though I believe in God above,
In His deep, holy, sacral love,

I must raise my fearful toasts
To all the intervening ghosts
Who cluster at my burning ear
To fuel my never-ending fear

The White Cockade

That my gain is all their loss,
What looks like gold to me is dross.
I shall not blame that hidden throng;
Who is the singer? Whose the song?

But if, my friend, you ask of me
Why I was cold in such degree,
It was no lack of love for you,
Not for the rest, that friendly few.

The ghost that on my brain intrudes
Is ghastly father of my moods.
I thank Christ's Father for His Grace
Of birthing me within my race,

But of Him also ask the boon
Of rising not from out my tomb.
To not before some child arise
And bring down fire from the skies.

For despite our era's refuse piled,
There yet are altars undefiled.
From them heedless of all vice
Yet pure arises Sacrifice.

Crowns and armor still remain
For mortal men, great risking pain,
Today might rude upon the Quest
Which pleases well our Divine Guest.

May my descendants not require
My ghost to light in them the fire
Which, reflection of Angelic light,
Will serve to pierce the darkest night.

Nocturne for the King of Saxony
19 March 1990

Majesty! Welcome to your halls,
   Site in former times of balls,
Feasts in honor of the Crown
   Your fathers wore in Dresden town.
After years of dirt and slag,
Again, watchtower flies your flag.

In these unroyal united states
   We cannot understand these fates
Whose fierce uncanny voices sing
   Return of Emperor and of King,
No matter! You may flow on tide
   Returning Europe's regal pride
So that every land and place
   May welcome back its regal race.

Our duty, which we may not shirk
   Is not to take this time to smirk
At thrones *we* may not sit upon -
   Lest Arthur rise in Avalon.
Majesty! Enjoy this day,
   While we pursue our darkened way.

AN AFTERTHOUGHT:

If you are reading these words, it may be safely assumed that you have read at least some of the poems and verse in this book. For that, you are thanked. But you may perhaps be a bit curious about the attitudes which gave rise to these efforts at verse.

We live in a time of uncertainty, or rapid change. Not merely of technologies and ideas, which have shifted throughout this century, but, as I write, in the political sphere. In this year of 1990, we are witnessing an apparent change as radical as those of 1918 and 1945; the demise of the Soviet Union as a major threat. The repercussions are everywhere, and no one knows what the shape of the world will be when the dust clears.

But history records many such shifts in the world of men. While important in the day-to-day conduct of affair, they are not immutable. No matter how earth-shaking these events appear, they are not permanent, and will one day affect man only in a distant, barely perceivable manner, There is more to life than these.

Despite the seeming chaos of this world, there is an order above, beyond, and throughout it. In the changing of the seasons, the nature of the heavens, in all creation, it may be seen. It is clearer yet in Man's art, music, legend, myth, and folklore. But it is most clearly seen in Revelation. To be more specific, in the doctrines and sacraments of Catholicism. The nature of this order is best exemplified, perhaps, in the old rites of Baptism of an infant, Consecration of a bishop, and Coronation of a king.

This order is today under attack, indeed, after being assaulted for several centuries it is almost invisible in the affairs of men. There is no admitted hierarchy or authority, the family means nothing, and politics are based entirely upon the pursuit of wealth, rather than the good. In terms of religion, the same thing has occurred, with increasing fury in the few years I have been alive. In place of the unchanging liturgies and doctrines of the Church, all is arranged at the whim of the clergy. Gone is the sense of the sacred, gone is the sense of objective truth, gone are eternal values.

So it is that my generation is one "lost in time and lost in space - and meaning." Between the eternal order earlier described, and the institutionalized disorder and anarchy of spirit which reigns today, we are suspended. Without examples, without encouragement from these generations which preceded us, we must somehow find our way back to that order. In this quest, our major weapon must be, perforce, the imagination,

Men like J.R.R. Tolkien have contributed mightily to this quest. In writings such as his we may see that love, honor, piety, truth, valour, and the like are not contradictory, but tightly united. The soul is naturally Christian, as Tertullian tells us, and so will respond to truth automatically - if the will is not malformed. Beauty, and that not least in literature, can help orient the soul in the proper manner. This is important today as never before, when the structures in Church and State point in quite an opposite direction.

Before the so-called Reformation, our ancestors evolved under the influence of the Faith as a society as perfect as anything human can be, a society which held as its ideal that same order in nature and supernature we have been discussing. This attempt was reflected in every aspect of its life, and in the Catholic and Orthodox cultures which were formed by it. Its imperfections were many and glaring, and its discomforts legion. But its ideals were aimed at God and reality, and its people were richer and spiritually healthier than we are. Not for them the modern ills of alienation and aimlessness! The Church existed to help men save their souls through the sacraments, and the State to aid the Church in her mission by enforcing justice, dispensing mercy, and accepting truth in the temporal sphere. At the junction of the two arose knighthood, whose code of Chivalry was certainly the best ethical system for men of action the world has yet seen.

But the Protestant revolt introduced a concept which has been the cause of much ruin, including that of our own, bloodiest of centuries. That is the idea that every individual may judge for himself what is true in the spheres of religion and morality, without reference to Divine Authority and Tradition. We today are so far involved in this idea that it seems reasonable to us. But attempt to apply it to science or finance and see what happens! Only the New Agers go far enough with the principle, declaring that they will create their own reality. If this sounds peculiar, remember that it is only the application of Luther's dictum of Private Judgment to all else besides religion. If consistency is praiseworthy, then the Protestants should laud and welcome the New Age.

From Luther's time to the present, his principle has gradually expanded its scope beyond religion, though not so completely as the Aquarians have done. Thus the essential unity of Christian Europe, the Holy Empire, the *Res Publica Christiana*, was dealt its deathblow in the Thirty Years War. Monarchy itself, and the sacral nature of the State was successively battered in 1789, 1830, 1848, and 1918. Despite occasional successes, like the Spanish Civil War, the Old Order was completely defeated in the military and political sense by 1945. With Communism triumphant in the East, continuing secularization and technologization in the religious and moral spheres advanced, resulting in the spiritual vaccum we presently enjoy in the West. The only area where some remnant of communion with the real order of things may still be experienced is in the artistic realm. This is the importance of men like Tolkien.

Or so it seems to me. But with such a worldview, you must not be surprised if your poet loves legendry, and herb-lore, and craft in artwork, and the Latin Mass, and folk customs of farm and wood. Neither must you be surprised if he despises the Catholic idiocies arising since Vatican II, or politicians who prate about the people and follow their own agenda, or standardization in anything.

My heroes are the men who fought for Christendom, like the Crusaders. Jacobites, Tories, Miguelists, Carlists, Legitimists - these attract my admiration. Whether one talks of Patrick Sarsfield at the Boyne, or Denikin on the Volga, or Jan Sobieski at Vienna, it is one conflict that he is speaking of, really.

That battle is not just military, of course. The Catholic Social theorists of the last and the early part of this century tried to apply the teachings of the Popes and the experience of Christendom to the modern world. Garcia Moreno, Fr. Coughlin, Dollfuss, and men like them showed that present-day society and economics can have some relation to reality, after all.

As a writer, though, it is the work of artists and philosophers in defending the right which has particularly inspired me. Chesterton, Belloc, Machen, Scott, Williams, and of course, Tolkien are a few of those who wrote in English who are of this breed. But Goerres, Chateaubriand, Novalis, De Maistre, Schlegel, and a host of others complement them in French and German; not least of whom is the towering figure of Franz von Baader. In other arts, the Pre-Raphaelite Movement, the Nazarene Brotherhood, the Blue Rider group, and William Morris' Arts-and-Crafts folk are all proponents of these ideals.

It will be readily apparent that there is here encompassed an enormous variety of artists. But despite their differences in style, all reflect to a greater or lesser degree that order. You will see it in Classicists like T.S. Eliot and Charles Maurras, and in Neo-Romantics like Stephen George's circle and the Inklings. So too in the political sphere this reflection is to be seen here and there in things as diverse as Solidarism, Distributism, Corporatism, and Guild Socialism. No one is perfect, and all the men and groups to which I have referred often did not live up to their ideals. But they at least had them, bright and shining as the sun on a pool in a green wood. We do not.

An Afterthought

At this point, gentle reader, you may be tempted (or someone you know may be tempted) to say "how dare you say such things, you reactionary dreamer!" Well, look at it this way. With an outlook like mine, an individual must come in contact on a daily basis with ideas that annoy him quite as much as his might annoy the reader. Can he, would he, should he demand of the holders of those opinions abject apologies for holding them? Since he does not, he tenders none, either. And, since the whole point of our present system is actually the creation of one's own reality, we have seen, who can blame him if he does so?

It may be objected that the poet's ideas are impractical, dreamy, and impossibly Romantic. Yes, well, maybe so. But practical, clear-eyed men have held sway for ever so long, and have only the present system to show for it. These practical men, both in Church and State, said, as an example, that Communism was a given - impervious to any change. Yet in this year of 1990 we see not merely its apparent demise, but arising from its ruins, the return of many groups and parties who yearn for the order we have looked at earlier: Monarchists, Clericals, Christian-Socials, and Traditionalists of all descriptions. As such folk have emerged from the wreck of the Soviet bloc, perhaps something similar may one day come from the stultified culture, abused environment, and graveyard of the unborn we call the West. At least, one can hope.

These then, are the attitudes which gave rise to the verses you have read. Perception and love of the Divine order of things, a sense of the supernatural, a preference for the colorful, are their traits. They have preserved in your poet a belief in the power of truth, goodness, and beauty, despite the proliferation of ugliness. I make no pretense of infallibility in the matter we have discussed, but I do claim a sense of taste, at least enough to discern where lies the good, the true, and the beautiful.

But if I have seen these items reflected in all the things we have just surveyed, they have been demonstrated to me by my friends. God has blessed me with quite a number of them, and all have been most helpful in the development of my poetic voice and vision. I wish to acknowledge here some of them - those who, unknowingly, contributed to or inspired the verse in this book. Most do not share all of my opinions, but then, love is rarely based on unanimity, as may be seen from any corporate boardroom. But they all share one trait, a trait which I wish at least to imitate. They are all questing for truth and beauty. In my own opinion, despite their wide variety and sometimes inimical interests, they are as grand a company as ever flourished this side of Camelot.

All of which having been said, it remains only to thank them. First of course, comes Ryan Brookhart, for his friendship as well as his strenuous artistic efforts on behalf of this book, and J. Fred Farrell, Jr. for his laudatory foreword;

The dedicands come next: Mr. Charl Van Horn, the "cher maitre" who taught me to write at school; Tim and Bonnie Callahan, who introduced me to the world of Tolkien, Lewis, and Williams, and who epitomise all that is best in a certain time; and Stephan, Baron Hoeller-Bertram, whose support sustained me in many a dark hour.

An Afterthought

Now we pay our respects to the dead friends whose example inspired me to do as they did: James Francis Cardinal McIntyre, Fr. Mark Falvey, S.J., Fr. Feodor Wilcock, S.J., Miss Octavia Curry (my Latin instructor), Bud and Anne Semco, and the fine actor, Mr. Henry Brandon.

To Dean McGovern, whose courage and nobility in the face of adversity have been a real light to me; Matt Hale, whose loyalty is extraordinary; Roberta "Chantal" Tropp, the soul of feminine elegance; Judith Richardson, whose wit and beauty conquer those who know her; Karen Semco, most wonderful of photographers and of friends; Mrs. Mary Pomerleau for her kind literary advice, and Peter McDonald, talented alike in acting and friendship; I am always indebted and wish I could repay them with more than a mention.

Bret and Maureen Herring, Brian and Eve Hansen, Gary and Beebe Frans (with my godson, Alexander Frans!), Delvis and Deborah Seda, and Robert and Maria Elena Kennedy also require more than a mere mention, for both the job of knowing them, and the chance to observe that odd phenomenon called married life.

Captain James and Laurie Herson, Alan Mather, Edward von Bluhm, and Ron Righter I have known since college, and they have me a better man thereby.

The divine Misses Tequila Mockingbird and Virginia O'Brien (the former of whom produced my other godson, Harley) continue to reflect in their own ways the wonder of Hollywood; Miss Arwen Goodknight continues to shed her beams upon the town of Altadena.

To Mr. Robbie Robertson, Mr. Tony Caruso, Mr. George Diestel and the past and present membership of the Masquer's Club also goes some of my gratitude, as well as to my "daughter," Jane Gartenmann.

One must not forget the White family, as well as their son Roger, who has left these shores for England. Nor can we leave out the "fearsome foursome" from Daniel Murphy High: Stewart Beckman, Gualtiero Negrini, John Garry, and Geoff Civello. Niel Citrin, marvellous editor that he is, ought not to go unmentioned, nor Peggy and Mike Dykes and Kirk Mulhearn. For that matter, it would be criminal to forget Jim Hill, his wife Donna, his mother Joanne, and his siblings Greg, Pat, Mike, Joe, and Margie - or Virginia and Teak Maas.

At New Mexico Military Institute, Col. Posz, Col. Limbaugh, and Col. Robbins must take their share. So too must General Riseley, Eileen and Frank Dill, and Chuck Underwood - to say nothing of the Bridge family and Col. Bartl.

Then there are other writers - Fr. Malachi Martin, Gary Potter, Richard and Silvana Cowden Guido, Farley Clinton, Drs. John and Hereward Senior, and Frederick Wilhelmsen - who have been both guides and models.

Harry and Jessica Dunn, Fairfax Bahr, Mark Lindquist, and Ajai Sahgal, each of them too terribly creative, must be thanked, as must Paul Lauer be. For that matter, the Register/Twin Circl gang: Fran Maier, Joop Koopman, Megan, John Prizer, Lori Seayer, M.L. Frawley, and the rest.

Nor must we leave out the Reverend Clergy: Fr. Francois LeBlanc, Fr. Paul Wickens, Fr. John Quinn, Fr.

John O'Connor, O.P., Fr. Flavian Wiillathgamua, C.M.F. and Fr. Mark Finan, S.J.

Lastly, my family really ought to be thanked, so here, then, is my tank you to my parents, Guy and Patricia Coulombe; my nephews, Guy, Charles, Phillip, Nicolas, and Albert Coulombe; my aunts, Virginia Barrett and Mary Henry; and my cousin, Dr. Albert R. Audet.

Doubtless, dear and gentle reader, this list seems obscenely long. In reality, it is far too short, and your versifier is only too aware of the many unpardonable omissions. To those whom he has missed, he can only say that, if God wills it, they will be properly commemorated in subsequent books.

Now my friends, our time together has come to an end. May we soon meet again!

AFTERWORD:
(Original Foreword)

Half a century ago, in the Poetry Room sequestered among the battlements of Widener Library overlooking the elms of Harvard Yard, I encountered the great poets of the English and French traditions. The memory of the aesthetic delight engendered by the contact with these word-artists is as vivid to my spirit as is the memory of the physical delight of effortlessly rowing a scull on the calm waters of the Charles River on a crisp New England October afternoon.

Good poetry can combine physical, mental, and spiritual delight when it springs from the inner soul of the poet. Eliot and Frost, Chaucer and Villon and Claudel show us in their works their aspirations and their limitations, their nobility and their defects. As editor of this collection of poems and verse by a distinguished young prose writer and lecturer Charles A. Coulombe, I have the opportunity to present for your consideration and appreciation a man who represents the best of young, contemporary Catholic writers.

Who is Charles A. Coulombe?
What is his background and training?
What are the wellsprings of his poetic inspiration?
What are the primary themes and motivations for his poems?
Do the felicitous phrase and the moving rhythm mark his presentation?

Does a sense of the human (and superhuman) drama and the seer's responsibility manifest itself in his work?

What enables him to have the breadth of world-view and depth of sensitivity to present his poetic vision?

Does he speak only to his contemporaries or does he have something to say to all who have eyes to see and ears to hear?

Who is this young and forceful writer?

Coulombe's Background

Charles Coulombe is a commanding personality, beyond his years. Of medium height and weight, he walks with the stride of an equestrian. Fluent in French and German, from the time he was nine he travelled extensively throughout the Americas and overseas. Though he is under thirty he has read many thousands of books in all fields, but especially in religion, poetry and literature, and political and military science. His daily reading includes many national and international periodicals. Because of an amazing memory recall, his erudition is remarkable.

Washington Irving, Edgar Allen Poe, Nathaniel Hawthorne and, more recently, H.P. Lovecraft and the Greyhaven Group of Diana Paxon and Paul Zimmer have been Coulombe's major American models in writing both prose and poetry. From England he takes Arthur Machen, G.K. Chesterton, Hilaire Belloc, and above all, J.R.R. Tolkien as influences. In philosophy he follows the great Franz von Baader.

His Schooling

His early education – except for two years spent in a public inner city school where he learned valuable lessons in the art of survival – was in the Catholic school system of the Los Angeles Archdiocese.

As a second-grader at the Blessed Sacrament School on Sunset Boulevard in Hollywood, he demonstrated a deep concern for order and orthodox behavior during a plebiscite conducted by the Immaculate Heart nuns who taught in the school. The nuns disobeyed their superior, the venerable James Cardinal McIntyre, the Archbishop of Los Angeles, by dropping their habits in favor of miniskirts and earrings. When the eight year-old Charles was asked why he did not vote in favor of the new dress, he replied, before the whole class, "Sister, a soldier has his uniform, a priest has his cassock, and a nun has her habit. If she doesn't want to wear it, she shouldn't be a nun." This sentiment was echoed by other in the school who asked, "Sister, if you won't obey the Cardinal, why should we obey you?"

During four years in the Archdiocesan High Schools he was taught by Dominican Fathers, Sacred Heart Fathers, and Xavierian Brothers. The religion courses included Bible Study (or Why Genesis Ain't So); Comparative Religions, complete with a fire worship service by a Zoroastrian priest; Marriage and the Family (or Whatever Your Conscience Tells You); and finally, Catholic Dogma taught from a Teilhardist text, *Christ Among Us*, written by a Paulist (now married), from which the Vatican later ordered the Imprimatur of Archbishop Gerety expunged.

Among the most fruitful of Coulombe's educational experiences were the two years that he spent at the New Mexico Military Institute in Roswell N.M. This formerly Cavalry school, with its motto of duty, honor, and achievement, called youth to high ideals in defense of Country under God. The Catholic Chaplain who had been a Cavalry officer during the War, preached on the Holy Eucharist, Mary, the Angels and Saints, the Holy Souls in Purgatory, the Rosary, Sin and true Catholic morality to the cadets at the required weekly Masses.

Under a distinguished Liberal Arts faculty – most notably, Mr. Charl Van Horn – Coulombe developed his prose and his poetic talents. At NMMI he spent as much time as possible on horseback and became a member of the Saunders Cavalry Troop. Among these cadets he developed enduring friendships which are recalled in his poem *In Memoriam Vini Antiqui*.

Coulombe's last two collegiate years were spent studying Political Science at California State University at Northridge.

The Wider World

To test his ambition to serve in the political scene, he enlisted as a Congressional Aide to a Representative in Washington. Although he enjoyed the balls and receptions along Embassy Row, his disillusionment with the field of national politics came to a head when, listening in the gallery to a discussion of a large Foreign Aid allotment, he heard an august Member of the House of Representatives ask the Speaker remind him of the continent where the country Angola was located. His final political activity was a failed effort to defeat an unworthy incumbent.

Coming from a family with four generations on the stage, he determined to try his hand at acting and was for a period of three years a stand-up comic in the clubs of the Hollywood scene. He was a prominent member of the most famous actor's club, the Masquers. Although his stint on the stage was an enjoyable time for him, he has often compared it to a diet of cotton candy.

After graduation from NMMI, Coulombe served in the California National Guard.

At present, Coulombe is a free-lance writer for newspapers and magazines in this country and overseas. His skills develops as a stand-up comic have been valuable to him on the lecture stage.

Everyman Today Call Rome

It was his first book, *Everyman Today Call Rome*, that brought to my attention the writing talents of the young author. Written when Coulombe had just turned 24, the book is a *cri de coeur* for a whole generation of young Catholics who because of the materialism and utter lack of Faith on the part of their parents, their teaching Sisters, their priests, and their bishops, were put out in a world of wolves without the strong armor of the Holy Faith.

National recognition of the intuitive genius of the young writer is to be found in the reviews of this book, as follow:

Malachi Martin, author of five *New York Times* bestsellers, wrote "Excellent, I say excellent."

Catholic Treasure wrote "A book for everyone. A refreshing antidote to the trivialized."

Fr. Enrique Rueda author and columnist wrote "It minces no words... a truly radical book... invaluable resource... inspirational and at the same time tough as nails."
The Homiletic and Pastoral Review praised the "Upbeat, blunt terms voicing deep thoughtfulness...to give their faith a boost."

Perhaps Gary Potter, veteran Catholic editor, saw most clearly the promise of Coulombe when he wrote in his column *Intra Urbem Extraque* "Mark the name of Charles A. Coulombe... Coulombe offers answers... He has to be kept poor and obscure if he stays to the course he has charted for himself with this book... What can await him, given the temper of the age, besides sacrifice and the kind of lacerating frustration that can come from knowing the answers this society needs for its largest questions, but is not willing to hear?"

His book has had wide circulation, not only throughout the United States and Canada but overseas in Great Britain and Australia and New Zealand.

Fidelity (of Australia) called *Everyman Today Call Rome* "Sensational... The book that can bring about a revolution for truth in the Church."

Christian Order of London said "A fighting book... Not a nice little pious book... He writes very well with plenty of drive, flair, and spiky humor... Irrepressible in his pokes at trendies... All can learn from it."

Coulombe has received hundreds of favorable letters- some most laudatory – not one unfavorable. He has made a point to answer each letter personally.

The White Cockade in its subjects, philosophy, and substance will show the attentive reader what motivates the author. It should also provide encouragement and answers for other young people.

The Inner Man

Having considered the background education and external influences on Charles A. Coulombe let us turn to a consideration of the inner man.

Coulombe is – at least in his writing and thought patterns – a child of his age. Born in the '60s under the aegis of Camelot, raise in New York and Los Angeles, tri-coastal in his 20's, a world traveler and bon vivant, military man, budding politico, a picketer for Catholic causes, actor and clubman, a rebel against Yuppyism, Charles can respond to all the calls of the under-thirties. With vast literary and intellectual interests he can look back to an ancestry that was activist and exploratory as well as religious, militant, and traditional.

Coulombe is as at ease with the King and Queen of Sweden at the Motion Picture Academy as with the Maitre d' and his favorite waiter Julius of the Beverly Hills Hotel Polo Lounge. The Sergeant-Major of his National Guard regiment called him the best officer that he had ever served under. His editors regard him as the conscience of their publications. He is a gifted raconteur of a myriad of "clean" stories; a singer of a thousand ballads and songs from Chaucer to Sam Cooke.

Loyalty and Chivalry

One who knows him well would say that the outstanding character trait is loyalty: loyalty to his Faith, his family, his schools, his comrades, his country, his traditions, and to all that has touched his heart. In Coulombe's mystique these loyalties are intertwined and, indeed, united.

For the Catholic our first devotion and loyalty is to Jesus Christ, our God and King; and since she has never been separated from her Divine Son, devotion to Him implies and leads to devotion to Mary the Mother of God and our Queen. The revelation of God and His Will for us is made known to us only in the Holy Church that He founded. The sanctification which opens to us the gates of Heaven is given to men only by the seven sacraments which the Church makes available.

Christian training in an orthodox Catholic family insured the full Faith to young Charles at a time when his schoolteachers – Sisters, Brothers and priests were presenting a perverted faith using such texts as the Teilhardist *Christ Among Us* (later condemned by the Vatican).

Family history recalled that the Coulombes bore on their coat of arms the crescent which showed that they had fought the Moslems during the Crusades to rescue the Holy Land.

A study of the history of Christendom led Coulombe to see in the code of Chivalry the highest expression of a Christian's life on earth. A militant Faith was in his bones. If the saying is true that "the pen is mightier than the sword" perhaps Coulombe in his literary defense of the Catholic Faith to which he has dedicated his life may do more than his predecessors to promote the Kingdom of Heaven.

The White Cockade

The poems in this collection have been loosely grouped in three sections: aspirations, observations, and conclusions. Because there is a continuity in Coulombe's thoughts and inspirations, the date of composition has been disregarded. Poems from his earliest period are found near those of more recent composition when the subject is similar. Some of the poems could be placed in any of the three categories.

My favorite poem is the one which leads to this collection, *The March Warden's Song*, because it best represents to me the loyal, militant yet solitary character of the author. The two following poems accent the loyalty to the Jacobite cause that has been characteristic of his ancestry. *Stabat Mater Dolorosa* was inspired by a visit to the Californian Mission of Nuesta Senora De Soledad, one of the chain of Spanish Missions founded by Blessed Junipero Serra, OFM.

Several poems such as *The Wild Hunt* take as their starting point the fantasy and horror tales and cinema which the young people of Coulombe's generation find so fascinating. Stephen King, Ray Bradbury, the Mythopoetic Society, the Greyhaven Group (Diana Paxon and Paul Zimmer), Steven Spielberg and other contemporary artists have exercised a strong influence on his writing. Even so, his own strong principles and loyalties stand out.

At the New Mexico Military Institute in Roswell, New Mexico, Coulombe encountered many who remain his closest friends and under expert instruction developed his literary skills. The section of the book called "observations" has many poems from this period. The leading poem *In Memoriam Vini Antiqui* was recently occasioned by a lecture visit to the Alma Mater.

"Conclusions" draws together the many threads that compose the tapestry of Coulombe's thought and life. As he "rides upon the Quest" he recalls "Ancestral blood" and European roots as well as "L.A.'s streets," Buzzard Bay, and "the strange New England of the soul."

His grandfather's recollections of the visit of Halley's Comet in 1910 accent the muted visit of 1987, which as an old man, he also witnessed. This led to the judgment, in *In the Year of the Comet*.

"This time the comment won't be so bright, it cannot pierce our modern night."

The Ghost Book ends this collection in deeply personal vein echoing the majestic *The March Warden's Song* which began the book.

As a poetic epilogue, Charles Coulombe has added a recently composed poem, *A Nocturne for the King of Saxony* as a final note of hope and a partial answer to the problems in the opening poem *The March Warden's Song*. It was composed as a result of the recent changes in Eastern Europe.

Ryan Brookhart, 24, who drew the pen-and-ink illustrations for the book has captured much of the spirit of Coulombe's poetry. We may expect great things in the future from his artistic talent.

As editor of this collection, I feel honored that I can let the literary public know the poetic talent of one who I regard as a "verray parfit gentil-knight."

J. Fred Farrell, Jr.
Original Foreword -1990

www.ingramcontent.com/pod-product-compliance
Lightning Source LLC
Chambersburg PA
CBHW031300290426
44109CB00012B/663